Original title:
The Seeker's Star

Author: Lan Donne
ISBN HARDBACK: 978-1-80561-209-4
ISBN PAPERBACK: 978-1-80561-770-9

A Dreamer's Map Through Galaxies

In the quiet of night,
Dreamers sketch their flight.
Stars like pearls in black,
Guiding souls on track.

Across the cosmic sea,
Wonders call to me.
Planets spin and glow,
In the stardust flow.

Every journey starts,
With hopeful hearts.
Maps made of delight,
Light the endless night.

Whispers in the breeze,
Poems in the keys.
Galaxies unfold,
Stories to be told.

Adventure awaits,
Beyond heaven's gates.
In dreams we do roam,
Finding our true home.

Lost in the Orbit of Hope

Caught in the swirl,
Of a bright, new world.
Doubts drift like dust,
In this orbit, trust.

Hope shines so bright,
In the darkest night.
Each star a promise,
Whispers of kindness.

We chase the unknown,
Through the seeds we've sown.
Our dreams start to soar,
On wings to explore.

With every heartbeat,
Challenges we greet.
Gravity can't bind,
The sparks of the mind.

Lost in a dance,
Life's wondrous chance.
Orbiting with grace,
Finding our place.

The Starry Guide of Heartfelt Wanderings

Beneath the vast sky,
Wanderers float high.
Stars twinkle and blink,
In silence, we think.

Guided by our dreams,
Through celestial beams.
Each journey we take,
Leaves a gentle wake.

Heartfelt whispers soar,
On the cosmos' floor.
Mapping out our fate,
As we navigate.

Every twist and turn,
With lessons to learn.
Constellations sigh,
As moments pass by.

The universe calls,
As adventure befalls.
In starlight we find,
The ties that bind.

Through the Veil of Starlight's Embrace

Veils of soft starlight,
Wrap the world in night.
Whispers in the air,
Carry dreams to share.

Through the endless space,
We find our own place.
Nebulas appear,
Like magic, they draw near.

In the shadow's gleam,
Life unfolds like a dream.
The cosmos reveals,
What our heart conceals.

Finding peace in flight,
Soaring to new heights.
With beauty around,
In freedom we're found.

Embraced by the night,
Hearts glow with delight.
Through the starlit streams,
We wander with dreams.

Questing for the Cosmic Key

Through endless night, the seeker roams,
Needing truth in celestial combs.
Each star a clue, a whispering tone,
Quesence beckons, guiding alone.

In shadows deep where dreams entwine,
Eclipsed by thoughts that brightly shine.
A journey far, yet close at heart,
The cosmic key, a work of art.

The void of space, a canvas vast,
A hint of hope, from ages past.
With every pulse, the universe sings,
Unveiling wonders that patience brings.

On stardust roads where spirits dance,
In twilight's glow, we take our chance.
To find that key of ancient lore,
Unlock the door, and so much more.

As comets blaze across the sky,
Our dreams take flight, we learn to fly.
In unity, we rise and soar,
The cosmic key reveals what's more.

Navigation through the Ether

In currents strange, the ships do glide,
Past swirling mists, where secrets hide.
With starlit maps in hand, we steer,
Seeking realms both far and near.

Galactic winds, they push and pull,
A dance of fate, both bright and dull.
Constellations whisper paths unknown,
In this grand voyage, we are not alone.

The ether hums a soothing song,
Filling hearts with a sense of belonging.
Through cosmic waves, our spirits blend,
The journey's end is just a trend.

With every pulse, the stars align,
Gracious signs in the great design.
As we embark, our souls take flight,
In navigation through the night.

To wander far is to explore,
The vast unknown, forevermore.
With every heartbeat, we embrace,
The beauty found in endless space.

Galaxy's Hidden Embrace

In shadows deep, the galaxy waits,
Veils of wonder, hidden gates.
A cosmic cradle, warm and bright,
Where dreams are born in starlit light.

With tender grace, the stars caress,
Infusing hearts with cosmic stress.
Spiraling close, we find our way,
In the embrace of night and day.

The pulse of time, a gentle guide,
Through endless realms, we glide and bide.
Each whisper in the void we trace,
A map of love, our sacred space.

In cosmic arms, we learn to trust,
Beyond the veil, in stardust rust.
Awakening dreams, once lost at sea,
In galaxy's embrace, we find the key.

With every glance at skies above,
We feel the tug of endless love.
Together bound, we navigate,
In the galaxy's embrace, we elevate.

Starbound Reverie

In dreams we tread on golden beams,
Where starlight weaves our deepest themes.
Each twinkle holds a story told,
In starbound reverie, we unfold.

With every heartbeat, constellations spark,
Illuminating paths through the dark.
In the soft hush of night's embrace,
We find our truth, our rightful place.

Whispers of worlds both near and far,
Guide our thoughts where wonders are.
In unity, together we rise,
As dreams take flight beneath vast skies.

Serenades of cosmic dance,
Inviting all to take the chance.
A tapestry spun in twilight's glow,
In starbound dreams, we come to know.

Through galaxies vast, we soar and drift,
In every heartbeat, we feel the lift.
With each new dawn, our spirits free,
In starbound reverie, we are truly me.

Quest for a Brighter Sky

In the quiet whispers of the night,
We seek the stars, our guiding light.
Beyond the shadows, hope takes flight,
To chase a dream, to find what's right.

Mountains high and valleys low,
Through trials faced, we learn and grow.
With every step, the winds bestow,
A path to take, a strength to show.

Eyes set firm on horizons wide,
With love and faith, we'll turn the tide.
Each heartbeat echoes, side by side,
In unity, our souls abide.

The sun will rise, dispelling fears,
With every dawn, a chance appears.
We'll dance with joy, dismiss our tears,
And celebrate the passing years.

So on we march, though skies are grey,
Hand in hand, we light the way.
Through storms and suns, come what may,
Together, we'll find a brighter day.

Radiance of the Unknown

In shadows cast by time's embrace,
We search for light, a sacred space.
With hearts alight, we dare to trace,
The paths unseen, adventures race.

What lies beyond the veil of night?
In whispers soft, the stars ignite.
The dreams we chase, a wondrous sight,
In every pulse, a gentle light.

From depths of dark, the echoes call,
A symphony that binds us all.
Through every rise and every fall,
We find our rhythm, heed the thrall.

With courage strong, we face the mist,
The mysteries, we can't resist.
Each moment felt, a lover's kiss,
In realms unknown, we find our bliss.

So take my hand, let's venture wide,
Together brave, on hope's wild ride.
In the unknown, our dreams abide,
A radiant path where we'll reside.

Celestial Echoes

Across the sky, the heavens sing,
With voices soft, their blessings bring.
In the twilight, dreams take wing,
In cosmic dance, our hearts will cling.

Each star a tale, a life once lived,
A thousand wishes, freely given.
In astral realms, we find the sieve,
To sift through light, our spirits driven.

Within the void, the whispers flow,
Celestial secrets, ebb and glow.
The past we cherish, the future we sow,
In echoes dancing, time we throw.

So gaze above, let wonder rise,
In every spark, the universe lies.
With open hearts, we claim the prize,
A tapestry spun in vast blue skies.

And as the night softly unfolds,
We find our place, our stories told.
In every shimmer, light converts gold,
In boundless dreams, forever bold.

Fragments of Lost Light

In the depths of night, we seek the glow,
The fragments shining, whispers low.
Each puzzle piece, a tale to show,
Of dreams forgotten, time's cruel flow.

Once bright and fierce, now dimmed and frail,
We wander through the shadowed veil.
In search of spark, we leave a trail,
Through memories wrapped in a wistful tale.

What once was clear, now fades away,
Yet echoes linger, here to stay.
In haunted dreams, we find our way,
As light returns to break the gray.

So gather close, the pieces small,
In unity, we'll rise and call.
For in the dark, we're never tall,
Together strong, we'll break the fall.

In lost light's grasp, we learn to find,
The beauty hidden, love entwined.
With every shard, the past aligned,
We weave a future, brightly designed.

Chasing Aurora's Secrets

In twilight's grace, we softly tread,
Where whispers dance, where dreams are fed.
The northern lights, a fleeting glance,
We chase the hues, in cosmic trance.

With secrets veiled in colors bright,
Each pulse of green, each flicker of light.
A journey whispers through the night,
As hearts ignite in pure delight.

The sky a canvas, vast and wide,
We wander close, with hope as guide.
Stars weave tales of long-lost years,
In silent prayers, we shed our fears.

We stand beneath the swirling glow,
In stillness, we embrace the flow.
The secrets held by nature's hand,
Awake the dreams we've yet to understand.

As morning breaks, the colors fade,
Yet in our hearts, the magic stayed.
With each new dawn, we pledge once more,
To chase the secrets life has in store.

Journey to the Luminous Heart

On paths unknown, we take our flight,
Beneath the stars, through the velvet night.
With each step taken, spirits rise,
Guided by dreams and open skies.

A heart that glows, a beacon bright,
Drawing us closer, igniting light.
Through valleys deep and mountains high,
We seek the warmth, where passions lie.

With every heartbeat, the journey starts,
Echoing whispers of loving hearts.
In harmony, we find our way,
As night transforms to glorious day.

In quiet moments, truth we find,
The luminous heart, forever kind.
With open arms, we pledge to share,
This radiant light, beyond compare.

As we embark on paths anew,
Together we shine, ever true.
A journey vast, forever bright,
To the luminous heart, our guiding light.

Celestial Compass

Beneath the dome of twinkling stars,
Our souls align, heal all the scars.
A compass forged in night's embrace,
It points the way to a sacred place.

In cosmic dance, we learn to trust,
In whispered winds, in stardust's lust.
Each moment leads, each heartbeat glows,
A path of light, where hope bestows.

The universe sings a melody,
Of mysteries wrapped in harmony.
With open hearts, we heed the call,
The celestial compass guides us all.

Through twilight's grace, we rise and soar,
Seeking the truth forevermore.
In every star, in every glance,
The compass spins, leading our dance.

With every step, a story we weave,
In celestial maps, we dare believe.
Together we journey, hand in hand,
With trust as our guide, we find new land.

Starlit Pathways

In fields of silver, dreams take flight,
Under the glow of gentle light.
With every star that lights the way,
We wander deeper, come what may.

Through dusky trails, our laughter flows,
In starlit pathways, love always grows.
With every step, our spirits sing,
Awash in joy, the night we bring.

The moon above, a guiding friend,
In shadows deep, the light transcends.
With every whisper carried near,
The night reveals what hearts hold dear.

Among the stars, we carve our dreams,
In cosmic streams, our hope redeems.
With open minds and daring souls,
We journey on, as stardust rolls.

And though the dawn will soon arise,
In morning's glow, our spirit flies.
For starlit pathways lead us true,
Forever chasing skies so blue.

In the Shadow of Luminaries

Under a sky so bright and vast,
Voices whisper tales from the past.
Stars like jewels, scattered with care,
Moonlit paths on a quiet air.

Guided by light in the darkened night,
Dreamers dance in the soft twilight.
In their glow, secrets unfurl,
Igniting hearts, they spin and twirl.

Constellations weave stories old,
Of lovers lost and heroes bold.
Every twinkle, a message sent,
In every shadow, a dreamer's bent.

With every sigh, a spark ignites,
A journey led by starry lights.
Under their watch, we'll find our way,
In the shadows of the cosmic play.

Together we'll rise, hand in hand,
In this celestial, radiant land.
With each dawn, new hopes arise,
In the shadow of luminaries' prize.

Starry-eyed Wanderer

On distant paths where starlight gleams,
A wanderer treads through midnight dreams.
With eyes aglow and spirit free,
Searching for magic, longing to see.

Mountains high and valleys low,
Every step, a tale to sow.
Chasing the skies with every breath,
In pursuit of wonders, defying death.

Whispers of galaxies call his name,
In the face of darkness, he lights a flame.
Through forests deep and rivers wide,
His heart ignites as he takes each stride.

He dances where the shadows meet,
In the silence, his dreams are sweet.
Among the stars, he's never alone,
In his chest, the universe is sown.

A starry-eyed wanderer, bold and bright,
Embarking on journeys through the night.
With every twinkle, his spirit flies,
Forever bound to the open skies.

The Infinite Horizon

Where land and sky in wonder blend,
There lies a path that has no end.
Oceans whisper to distant shores,
In the horizon, adventure soars.

The sun dips low in a golden hue,
Painting dreams in vibrant blue.
With every wave, new hopes arise,
A canvas brushed with endless skies.

Mountains roll like waves of time,
Each peak tells tales in whispered rhyme.
Through valleys deep, where shadows play,
We journey forth, come what may.

Stars emerge as the daylight fades,
Lighting paths where the heart parades.
In the vastness, we seek our place,
Finding solace in nature's embrace.

The horizon beckons, a siren's call,
Inviting the brave to test it all.
With every step, a new world's born,
In the infinite horizon, we are reborn.

Celestial Blessings

In the quiet of the starry night,
Whispers of magic take to flight.
Celestial blessings dance in the air,
Wrapping the world with a tender care.

Moonbeams fall like silver threads,
Weaving dreams on quiet beds.
Each star a wish waiting to bloom,
In the shadows, dispelling gloom.

The cosmos sings a lullaby sweet,
Guiding souls with its rhythmic beat.
In the stillness, hearts unite,
Bathed in the glow of soft starlight.

Every heartbeat a pulse of grace,
In the universe's warm embrace.
With every sigh, we rise and sway,
Under the blessings that light our way.

Celestial wonders fill the sky,
With open hearts, we learn to fly.
In this cosmic dance, we find our peace,
Embraced by love, our souls release.

Wandering Light

In the hush of the night, I roam,
Beneath a blanket of stars, my home.
Radiance flickers in soft, sweet flight,
Guiding my heart with its gentle light.

Through shadows deep and pathways wide,
I follow the glow of the moon's soft tide.
Whispers of hope in the velvet air,
The warmth of the light, my silent prayer.

Each step I take, the world feels bright,
As I chase the dreams that dance in sight.
Every flicker a promise, a guiding spark,
Illuminating the way through the dark.

Time drifts along like a river's flow,
With wandering light, my spirit can grow.
The journey unfolds with each fading star,
Leading me onward, no matter how far.

So I wander beneath the celestial dome,
Embracing the path that feels like home.
For in every gleam, and every flight,
I find myself lost in wandering light.

Celestial Quest

In velvet skies where the galaxies spin,
I seek the echoes that lie within.
Stars align on a cosmic thread,
Charting the path where the brave have tread.

Galactic whispers in the still of night,
Calling to dreamers who chase the light.
Planets shimmer with secrets untold,
In the heart of darkness, I am bold.

With stardust wings, I soar through space,
Each constellation a sacred place.
The universe sings in tones so sweet,
Inviting the weary to dance on their feet.

In this vast expanse, my spirit's free,
On a quest for wonders, eternally.
Through cosmic seas and nebula's hue,
The heart of the stars calls out anew.

So I traverse the heavens with grace,
Embracing the mysteries I long to trace.
For in this quest, I find my truth,
A celestial journey that knows no youth.

In Search of Distant Dreams

Across the fields where the wildflowers sway,
I wander softly, lost in play.
Distant dreams weave through the gentle breeze,
Whispering tales of hope and peace.

Mountains rise like giants of old,
Guardians of secrets waiting to be told.
With every step, my spirit takes flight,
Chasing reflections of shimmering light.

Oceans beckon with their soothing songs,
In their depths, I've always belonged.
Searching the horizon where the sky meets sea,
For the distant dreams that still whisper to me.

Through valleys deep and forests wide,
In nature's embrace, I confide.
The beauty I find ignites my soul,
Each fleeting moment, a chance to be whole.

So I roam on, with heart open wide,
In search of dreams I can no longer hide.
For within the distance, there lies my fate,
Where every heartbeat reverberates.

In this journey, I find my way,
With distant dreams, come what may.
In the tapestry of night, I'm aware,
Every thread weaves a story, rare.

Guiding Light at Dawn

As dawn breaks through the shroud of night,
A tender glow ignites the fight.
Softly emerging, the sun ascends,
Bringing hope and warmth, the night it mends.

Colors splashed upon the waking sky,
A canvas painted as moments fly.
Each ray a reminder, a gentle nudge,
For the heart that trembles, it will not judge.

In the morning's embrace, shadows retreat,
A promise of courage, fresh and sweet.
With every heartbeat, the day unfolds,
Cascading stories waiting to be told.

The world awakens with a sigh of peace,
Every challenge faced leads to release.
Guiding light at dawn, steadfast and true,
Ignites the spirit, and dreams pursue.

So greet the sun with a heart that's brave,
For in every dawn, a new path we pave.
With joyous whispers carried on air,
The guiding light at dawn always cares.

As the day blooms bright with endless grace,
We march on boldly, leaving no trace.
For every sunrise tells us anew,
The guiding light is forever true.

Guiding Light in Abyssal Night

In shadows deep where silence calls,
A flicker gleams, a beacon small.
Each whispered hope in darkness blooms,
A guiding light through hollow plumes.

Lost spirits roam, their hearts entwined,
With fragile dreams, they seek, they find.
The light persists, a steady flame,
In depths of night, it speaks your name.

The stars above may seem so far,
Yet from your heart, they are not spar.
With every step, the path appears,
A dance of fate, it calms your fears.

The weight of doubt may drag you low,
But in the night, the strong will grow.
For every shadow has its fight,
And darkness yields to the bold light.

So trust the glow that you can see,
A guide for all who long to be.
In abyssal night, you will ignite,
Your spirit's strength, your guiding light.

Celestial Quest of the Wandering Soul

Through cosmic seas where stardust flows,
A wandering soul seeks what it knows.
With every glance at distant spheres,
Its journey thrives, eclipses fears.

In astral winds, the whispers rise,
A quest for truth beneath the skies.
The constellations weave their tales,
Of ancient myths, and starlit trails.

Each heartbeat drums a traveler's song,
In endless night, the soul belongs.
Embracing change with open arms,
It dances free through cosmic charms.

For in the void, possibility shines,
A tapestry of fates entwined.
With every star a guiding spark,
Illuminates the paths made dark.

So let your spirit roam the night,
In quest for all that feels so right.
The universe is vast and grand,
A sacred call, you'll understand.

Illuminated Paths of the Intrepid Dreamer

In twilight realms where visions merge,
The dreamer walks with heart ablaze.
Each step a stroke on canvas bright,
Creating worlds that mock the night.

Through shadows thick, the courage grows,
A tale of strength that only flows.
Every stumble turns to grace,
An illuminated, sacred space.

With hopeful eyes, the dreamer strives,
To craft the truths where freedom thrives.
In every heartbeat, whispers call,
A journey shared—embrace it all.

The paths may twist, but never end,
On courage born, dreams can transcend.
With every canvas, every hue,
A symphony of life comes through.

So boldly tread where few have dared,
In every moment, dreams are shared.
Illuminate with passion bright,
The paths you carve, your endless flight.

A Flicker in the Cosmic Dark

In cosmic dark where silence reigns,
A flicker sparks, a hope remains.
Through boundless space, it dares to fly,
In the vast void, it seeks the why.

Each star a dream, a story's start,
A luminous beat of every heart.
Though shadows loom, unseen, unfelt,
Within the dark, a warmth is spelt.

The flicker dances, whispers low,
A secret shared, an ember's glow.
In infinite night, it finds its way,
A promise held in starlit play.

Across the heavens, believed afar,
Each light a tale, each tale a star.
In cosmic dark, together we rise,
For every flicker softly ties.

So hold the light within your soul,
Let it shine bright, make you whole.
In the cosmic dark, we'll stand apart,
Together bright, a flicker's heart.

Celestial Hymn

In the night, stars softly gleam,
Whispering tales of a distant dream.
Moonlight dances on silver streams,
Guiding our hearts with celestial beams.

Constellations weave a timeless song,
Echoing where the lost belong.
Each note drifts, serene and strong,
In this vast night, we find our throng.

Clouds drape low, a gentle sigh,
As shadows flicker, and crickets cry.
Nature's chorus fills the sky,
Under the watch of the endless high.

Winds carry secrets, whispered low,
Through trees that sway, in moonlit glow.
They speak of love that we all know,
In this sacred space where dreams flow.

With every heartbeat, starlight beams,
In this moment, nothing's as it seems.
We drift along on twilight's seams,
Lost forever in celestial themes.

Twilight's Embrace

Beneath the sky painted in hues,
Twilight whispers, a gentle muse.
Shadows stretch as daylight dues,
Embracing night with the dawn's excuse.

Stars awaken in velvet skies,
Glimmers of truth, no disguise.
Time trickles softly, the heart complies,
In twilight's hold, the spirit flies.

A chill in the air, a sweet caress,
As day concedes to night's finesse.
Moonlight's kiss, a soft redress,
In the quietude, we find our press.

Whispers of dreams float on the breeze,
Twirling silently through the trees.
In this magic, our hearts find ease,
As twilight wraps us, like a tease.

Moments linger in this embrace,
As shadows play, a timeless chase.
Beneath the stars, we find our place,
In twilight's arms, a fleeting grace.

Veil of Celestial Dreams

Underneath the cosmic veil,
Whispers of dreams begin to sail.
Stars ignite in hues so pale,
Guiding us through this wondrous trail.

In the silence, secrets hum,
With every heartbeat, magic comes.
We dance to rhythms, soft and dumb,
Through night's embrace, we overcome.

Nebulae swirl in colors bright,
Painting the canvas of the night.
In the stillness, holds delight,
A dreamer's world, a pure invite.

Each twinkle tells a story spun,
Of distant worlds where hope runs.
Under the gaze of the evening sun,
Our spirits soar, forever one.

A lullaby, the night sings sweet,
As stardust dances at our feet.
In this realm, our dreams complete,
In celestial arms, we find our seat.

Night's Enigmatic Glow

In the depths of night's allure,
Mysteries dwell, rich and pure.
Beneath shadows, secrets stir,
In the quiet, our hearts confer.

Lucid dreams drift through the air,
Hints of magic, bold yet rare.
Stars above, a cosmic flare,
In night's embrace, we lay bare.

A shimmering path of silver light,
Guides us gently through the night.
While whispers weave a soft delight,
In enigmatic shadows, we take flight.

Each heartbeat aligns with the moon,
As night's sweet song begins to croon.
Timeless echoes, a haunting tune,
In this stillness, we are immune.

Lost in the glow, we find our way,
Each flicker ignites a new play.
In the hush, we choose to stay,
In night's embrace, come what may.

Mystic Gleams

In twilight's grasp, the shadows dance,
A whisper calls, inviting chance.
With echoes soft, the night unfolds,
Unraveling tales that time upholds.

Beneath the moon, the secrets rest,
In silver light, the world is blessed.
A gleam of hope in every sigh,
As dreams take flight, into the sky.

The stars align, a cosmic song,
Embracing hearts as they belong.
Each flicker tells of paths untold,
In mystic realms where love is bold.

Through veils of dusk, a journey stirs,
With every beat, the heartbeat purrs.
In twilight's hue, we find our way,
As night transforms to break of day.

So let us wander, hand in hand,
Toward the dreams we softly planned.
In mystic gleams, our spirits soar,
Forever seeking, evermore.

Embraced by Starlight

In quiet nights, when shadows creep,
The world is hushed, as dreams take leap.
With starry ties that softly sway,
We find our hearts, no words to say.

The sky, a canvas; the moon, a muse,
Each twinkle whispers, life's sweet fuse.
In silver beams, our worries fade,
As hopes arise, unafraid, unmade.

Embraced by starlight, souls entwined,
In cosmic dance, our fates aligned.
With every pulse, the night unfolds,
A tapestry of dreams retold.

Through constellations, silent vows,
We chase the light, beneath the brows.
As galaxies twirl, our spirits lift,
In boundless love, the greatest gift.

In this embrace, we lose the fight,
To time and space, our endless flight.
With whispered wishes, hearts ignite,
Forever cherished, embraced by starlight.

Solstice of the Soul

In shadows deep, the stillness waits,
As seasons turn, we meet our fates.
With every breath, a purpose found,
In solstice whispers, love unbound.

As daylight wanes, the fire glows,
Illuminating paths we chose.
In fleeting moments, truth appears,
To guide us through our hopes and fears.

The sun and moon, in harmony,
Bestow their grace, a symphony.
With light and dark, we intertwine,
In solstice tides, your heart in mine.

Through winter's chill and summer's blaze,
We journey forth, in sacred praise.
Embracing change, we stand as one,
In soul's solstice, we have begun.

So let the seasons mold our days,
In every challenge, love displays.
With open hearts, our spirits whole,
We celebrate the solstice of the soul.

Chasing Infinity

In distant dreams, where whispers blend,
We chase the light, around the bend.
With every heartbeat, we ignite,
In endless quest, through day and night.

The universe stretches far and wide,
In galaxies where passions bide.
With every step, we dare to see,
What lies beyond, our destiny.

Through cosmic realms, with open eyes,
With hope as wings, we learn to rise.
In chasing infinity, we find,
A world of wonders, unconfined.

With each horizon, new paths gleam,
A tapestry of light, a dream.
In every shimmer, souls collide,
With love as anchor, heart as guide.

So let us fly, with hearts ablaze,
In chasing infinity, we raise.
With hands joined tight, we seek and roam,
In every chapter, we find our home.

Luminous Pilgrimage

Beneath the twilight's glow, we tread,
On paths where ancient whispers spread.
Each step a journey, faint yet bright,
Towards the dreams that spark the night.

Stars above guide our wayward feet,
In a dance where earth and cosmos meet.
With every heartbeat, we ascend,
To realms where time and space transcend.

The moonlight bathes our weary souls,
As we traverse these endless shoals.
In silent prayers, our hopes we weave,
Trusting the light that we believe.

Through valleys deep and mountains tall,
In the embrace of night, we hear the call.
A luminous thread connects us all,
In this pilgrimage, we rise, we fall.

At dawn, our shadows kiss the day,
The stars retreat, and dreams give way.
Yet in our hearts, the glow remains,
A luminous fire that love explains.

Harmony of the Starlit Sky

In the quiet night, the stars align,
Whispers of cosmos in a dance divine.
Harmony sings from skies so wide,
Where secrets of the universe abide.

Constellations weave their stories bright,
Guiding lost souls through the velvet night.
Each twinkling light a tale to share,
In the symphony of the fateful air.

Galaxies swirl in a cosmic embrace,
Echoes of time in a timeless space.
With every breath, we feel their grace,
A harmony that time cannot erase.

Under this dome, we find our place,
A tapestry woven of love and grace.
In the starlit sky, our spirits soar,
Resonating with the universe's core.

As dawn approaches, the night will fade,
Yet in our hearts, the harmony stayed.
For in this sky, we've touched the divine,
Our souls forever in cosmic design.

Navigating Cosmic Currents

Drifting through the void, we find our course,
On waves of light, a celestial force.
With stardust dreams and comets' tails,
We ride the cosmic winds, where wonder prevails.

Planets spin in a silent waltz,
Time and space, intertwined by default.
With every heartbeat, the universe sings,
Guiding our journey on ethereal wings.

Through nebulous realms, we boldly glide,
Embracing the mysteries we cannot hide.
In cosmic currents, we learn to flow,
Finding our way where the galaxies glow.

Transcending bounds of the known and real,
In the vastness, there's so much to feel.
Navigating stars, our spirits align,
In this journey, we become the divine.

As horizons shift and new worlds rise,
We embrace the changes, embracing the skies.
With hearts wide open, we sail anew,
Navigating cosmic currents, ever true.

Reflections on the Dawn

In the hush of night, dreams softly fade,
As dawn unfolds in a golden cascade.
Light spills gently on the slumbering earth,
A reminder of hope, a promise of birth.

Each ray a whisper, a secret shared,
Illuminating paths that life has bared.
Reflections dance on the water's face,
In this quiet moment, we find our grace.

The world awakens, colors burst forth,
As the sun ascends to reclaim its worth.
With every heartbeat, a new story begins,
In the warmth of dawn, where life truly wins.

Birdsong fills the air, a sweet refrain,
Celebrating the light that washes the pain.
Through the lens of morning, we see anew,
In reflections of dawn, memories accrue.

So let us embrace each sparkling hour,
Finding solace in the sunlight's power.
In this golden glow, we transcend the night,
Reflections on the dawn, our spirits in flight.

Illuminated Yearnings

In the quiet depths of night,
Whispers of dreams take flight,
Stars twinkle with gentle grace,
Guiding hearts to their rightful place.

Crimson hues wash the dawn,
Painting skies with a hopeful song,
Each ray a tender embrace,
Awakening love in every space.

Beneath the moon's silver gaze,
We wander through enchanted maze,
Yearning to touch the divine,
With each moment, our souls entwine.

In the garden of silent wishes,
Where the heart's pulse softly swishes,
Joy blooms like flowers in spring,
Fulfilling every longing.

A tapestry woven of light,
Threads of hope shining bright,
In every heart, a spark remains,
Illuminating all our pains.

Astral Pursuit

Chasing the glow of distant stars,
Mapping dreams with cosmic bars,
Where shadows dance and fantasies sway,
In the silence, we find our way.

Glimmers of truth pierce the night,
Each heartbeat a fluttering light,
Spiraling down the celestial path,
Dancing through the universe's wrath.

Beneath the expanse, our wishes soar,
In the stillness, we seek for more,
Whispers echo from astral seas,
Guiding us with a gentle breeze.

Through galaxies, we spin and twine,
Every moment, a sacred sign,
In the vastness, we learn to trust,
Chasing starlight, as we must.

In the vast void, our dreams ignite,
Creating hope from endless night,
With each pulse, a promise renewed,
In this journey, our spirits brewed.

The Void's Radiant Promise

In the silence of the empty space,
Lies a promise, a gentle trace,
Carved in shadows, pure and bright,
A beacon glimmers in the night.

Through the chasm, we wander far,
Searching for the guiding star,
Each echo speaks of dreams long passed,
In the void, our hopes hold steadfast.

Whispers tell of tales untold,
Of journeys marked by heart and bold,
With every heartbeat, we collide,
As we traverse the cosmic tide.

In the dark, we find our way,
Through the struggles, we learn to sway,
The radiant glow, our hearts ignite,
Filling the void with love's pure light.

A tapestry of souls entwined,
With every moment, hearts aligned,
In this vastness, we are whole,
Together we heal, body and soul.

Light's Labyrinth

In a maze of shimmering beams,
We wander through enchanted dreams,
Each corner holds a secret thread,
Guiding us where angels tread.

Through the labyrinth, our spirits dance,
In every glance, a fleeting chance,
To find the path that leads us home,
In unity, we are never alone.

The walls echo with laughter sweet,
In this journey, our hearts beat,
With love as the compass, brightly cast,
Drawing us forward, unbound, unpast.

In the heart of light, shadows fade,
Illuminated truths are laid,
With each step, a new vision gleams,
Within the labyrinth of our dreams.

Together we seek, together we strive,
In the maze where the spirit thrives,
With radiant light, our fates we weave,
In love's embrace, we truly believe.

Threads of Cosmic Wonder

In the fabric of the night,
Stars weave dreams with silver light.
Galaxies spin, a dance so grand,
Each thread tells stories, hand in hand.

Between the wonders, deep and vast,
Echoes of the future and the past.
Celestial whispers paint the skies,
In every spark, a soul that flies.

Nebulas bloom, in colors bright,
A tapestry of dark and light.
Every shimmer holds a key,
Unlocking secrets, wild and free.

Planets hum a gentle tune,
Orbits guided by the moon.
In the silence, beauty sings,
As the universe of wonder springs.

So gaze upon the night's embrace,
Find your heart within this space.
In every star, a wish resides,
Threads of cosmic wonder as our guides.

A Star's Gentle Caress

A flicker in the velvet deep,
A gentle glow, where wishes leap.
Stars awaken hearts with grace,
Bestowing peace in their embrace.

Moonlit sighs upon the sea,
A tender touch, so wild and free.
Shadows danced in silver light,
Love ignites as day turns night.

The quiet hum of twilight's breath,
Whispers softly of life and death.
In every twinkle, hope is spun,
As dreams unfold, two become one.

Hearts align like constellations,
In the universe of vibrations.
A star's caress, a binding fate,
In cosmic warmth, we contemplate.

So let your spirit soar and play,
In the tranquil light, drift away.
For every star is a guiding flame,
A gentle caress that calls your name.

Through the Veil of Night

Through the veil of night we roam,
Among the stars, we find our home.
The cosmos sings in muted tones,
Where secrets lie in ancient stones.

In shadows deep, the dreams take flight,
Exploring realms far from the light.
Mysteries swirl in the darkened air,
Inviting us to wonder and dare.

Galactic rivers flow with grace,
Carving paths through timeless space.
The universe, a canvas wide,
Paints our stories as we glide.

With every heartbeat, stardust crumbles,
In the silence, our spirit humbles.
Together we weave through the unknown,
Finding solace in the celestial throne.

So let's embark on this wondrous quest,
Through the veil, we find our best.
In the arms of night, we'll entwine,
In cosmic beauty, we'll resign.

Whispers in the Celestial Winds

Whispers glide on cosmic streams,
Through the void, the starlight beams.
Voices soft as twilight's sigh,
Carrying secrets from the sky.

In a dance of shimmering grace,
Galaxies twirl in endless space.
Every breath a tale unfolds,
In the silence, the universe holds.

Comets race with a fiery glow,
Chasing dreams that ebb and flow.
In the symphony of night's embrace,
We find our place in time and space.

Echoes of eternity's song,
Remind us where we all belong.
Bound by threads of light and air,
Connected by the stars we share.

So listen close, to winds that call,
In the celestial realm, we'll never fall.
In this vast expanse, our spirits blend,
Whispers of the universe, forever a friend.

The Dreamer's Beacon

In twilight realms where shadows play,
A beacon glows, guiding the way.
Whispers of hope in the midnight air,
Dreamers gather, hearts laid bare.

Stars above twinkle bright and clear,
Echoes of wishes, soft and near.
A path illuminated by inner fire,
In the stillness, we reach higher.

Through labyrinths of thought we roam,
Each dream a step, leading us home.
In the silence, we find our song,
With every heartbeat, we grow strong.

Beneath the moon's gentle caress,
We shed our worries, embrace the rest.
Together we rise, hands intertwined,
In this dance of souls, perfectly aligned.

A tapestry woven in shades of night,
Each thread a vision, bold and bright.
As dawn breaks, our dreams take flight,
We are the beacon, casting light.

Ethereal Guidance

In realms where the shadows softly play,
Ethereal guides lead the way.
With wings of light, they lift the soul,
Whispering secrets, making us whole.

Through winds of change, they softly call,
Inviting us to rise, never fall.
In the stillness, their voices sing,
Harmonies of hope the heart can bring.

Moments of magic, woven tight,
In each heartbeat, they ignite the night.
A dance of spirit, so pure and free,
No chains can hold our destiny.

With courage born of stardust dreams,
We navigate the flowing streams.
Together we journey, never apart,
In the tapestry of each heart.

Glimmers of wisdom in every sign,
Guiding us gently, through the divine.
With every step, we trust the signs,
In the dance of life, our spirit shines.

Threads of Luminescence

In the quiet hours, we weave our fate,
Threads of light, intertwine and create.
Illuminated paths, through shadows they break,
Stitches of hope in every mistake.

Colors of dreams, vibrant and bright,
A tapestry formed in the heart of night.
Each thread a story, each color a song,
In the fabric of time, we all belong.

With hands of wonder, we craft our way,
Through laughter and tears, night and day.
Ebbing and flowing, with love we connect,
In the loom of life, we reflect.

Glowing threads shimmer, softly entwined,
Guiding lost souls to the light they find.
With every tug, a reminder appears,
To dance through the shadows, to face all fears.

As dawn emerges, the colors ignite,
The threads we have woven, a beautiful sight.
Together we rise, a radiant show,
In this world of threads, let our essence flow.

Celestial Fables

In the sky's embrace, stories unfold,
Celestial fables, timeless and bold.
Starry-eyed children of the night,
Listening close to the whispers of light.

Each constellation, a tale to be told,
Legends of love, of bravery, and gold.
Sketches of heroes, of battles fought,
In the canvas of space, their lessons are caught.

Moons weave tales of soft silver glow,
Guiding the dreamers where rivers flow.
Wonders unravel with every gaze,
In the starlit theatre, lost in a haze.

Every comet, a fleeting spark,
Dances through darkness, igniting the dark.
With each wish cast upon its tail,
Hopes and dreams set forth to sail.

As dawn breaks, the stories remain,
Celestial whispers, joy and pain.
In the tapestry of sky so vast,
We hold the fables of ages past.

Lost in Transcendence

In the whispers of the night,
Where stars and dreams unite,
I float on clouds of silver light,
Lost in time, in endless flight.

Echoes from a distant past,
Moments fleeting, shadows cast,
I search for peace that seldom lasts,
In the cosmos, vast and fast.

Above the realms of earthly bound,
In the silence, truth is found,
I dissolve into sounds profound,
Where inner peace and love resound.

Each breath a step to freedom's gate,
Navigating through fate's slate,
In this journey, I relate,
Transcendence calls, I contemplate.

A spark ignites the cosmic dance,
In the universe, I take a chance,
Lost in thoughts, a mystic trance,
In the depths of existence, I glance.

A Shimmer Among Shadows

In the dim of twilight's embrace,
Flickers light with gentle grace,
A shimmer dances, finding space,
Among the shadows, leaves no trace.

Whispers weave through the night air,
Secrets shared, souls lay bare,
Amongst the darkness, we declare,
Hope will rise, beyond despair.

Glimmers of truth in moonlit sighs,
Reflecting dreams that never die,
A beacon where the heart complies,
In shadow's depth, our spirit flies.

Every flicker tells a tale,
Of those who dared, who chose to sail,
Through tempests fierce, they shall prevail,
A shimmer's light, our holy grail.

In the dance of darkness, we find,
A luminous thread, gently entwined,
With courage bold, and hearts aligned,
A shimmer among shadows combined.

Footprints on Cosmic Sands

Beneath a sky of endless night,
Footprints left in stardust bright,
Tracing paths of dreams in flight,
On cosmic sands, pure delight.

Each grain a story, every step,
The universe sings as we prep,
For journeys deep, where secrets kept,
In the astral sea, we are adept.

Wonder glimmers in the void,
Stars like gems, bright and overjoyed,
In silent space, hearts are deployed,
Footprints fade, yet love's employed.

Navigation through uncharted skies,
With every leap, our spirit flies,
In the dance of worlds, we realize,
Footprints vanish, but never dies.

In the vastness, we belong,
Sailing crisp winds, a cosmic song,
Forever linked, forever strong,
On sands of time, we carry on.

Illuminated Horizons

At dawn, the world begins to wake,
Colors painted, a silent quake,
Illuminated horizons break,
With every light, our fears forsake.

From shadows deep, hope emerges,
As golden rays draw life's surges,
Across the land, the spirit purges,
In nature's grasp, our heart converges.

Mountains rise, kissed by the sun,
Every peak a race to run,
Illuminated paths have begun,
In unity, our voices spun.

With every step, the sky expands,
Embracing peace with open hands,
In ever-changing, shifting lands,
Illuminated dreams, our plans.

Through whispers of the morning light,
We dance together, future bright,
In harmony, we chase the sight,
Illuminated horizons, our right.

The Compass that Leads to Infinity

In hands it rests, a guide unknown,
Pointing paths, through skies we've flown.
With every turn, new worlds unfold,
The heart ignites, as dreams take hold.

Unraveled maps of starlit dreams,
Charting courses of silver beams.
A whisper soft, in twilight's call,
Leading us through the cosmic hall.

In whispers of the winds so free,
The compass sings a melody.
Through azure seas and boundless night,
Our spirits soar in the endless light.

The journey's long, yet time can bend,
With every star, our souls will mend.
In distant realms, we'll surely find,
The truths that live within the mind.

So take this compass, dear and true,
Embrace the paths that call to you.
For every step, a story spun,
Infinity waits for everyone.

Luminescence of the Adventurous Spirit

A light ignites within the brave,
Unearthed in depths, where dreams can pave.
With every heartbeat, courage grows,
As wild winds dance, and wonder flows.

Mountains high and rivers wide,
The spirit thrives, no need to hide.
In shadows cast by moonlit beams,
We chase the echo of our dreams.

Through forests dense and valleys deep,
Awakening secrets we must keep.
Each step a spark, each breath a flame,
In adventures bold, we make our name.

Together with the stars aligned,
Our journey paints what's undefined.
With laughter ringing in the night,
We'll weave our stories, bright and tight.

So let us roam, let spirits soar,
In every heartbeat, we'll explore.
Through luminescent paths we trek,
Where love and wonder intersect.

Dance of Lights in the Night's Embrace

The sky ignites, a canvas wide,
Where dreams and stars in unison glide.
Each twinkle tells a story bright,
In the dance of lights, we find our flight.

Beneath the moon's soft, silver gaze,
We wander lost in evening's haze.
The constellations gently sway,
Guiding the hearts that roam astray.

With every pulse, the shadows play,
As night unfolds what dreams convey.
In whispers soft, the cosmos calls,
As we surrender to its thralls.

With laughter shared and secrets spun,
In this embrace, we come undone.
In rhythms sweet, our spirits rise,
Dancing like fireflies in the skies.

So let the night cradle our fate,
In every twirl, new worlds await.
A tapestry woven, pure delight,
In the dance of lights, we claim our night.

A Voyage to the Celestial Horizon

Set sail for realms where stars are born,
In oceans vast, where dreams are worn.
With every wave, a tale unfolds,
The horizon whispers, fate beholds.

Through tempest storms and skies ablaze,
We journey forth through endless maze.
The compass points to skies so bright,
In pursuit of wonders, day and night.

With sails of hope, we glide through time,
In perfect rhythm, hearts in chime.
To realms where sunlight meets the sea,
A voyage calls, we're wild and free.

With every star that lights the way,
Our aspirations boldly sway.
The horizon beckons, just ahead,
Our spirits rise where dreams are led.

So venture forth, with love as guide,
In every heartbeat, let dreams ride.
For on this voyage, fate aligns,
To worlds of wonder, our heart entwines.

Elysian Realms of Radiance

In gardens where the golden light flows,
Whispers of joy in the sweet air glows.
Laughter dances on the breeze so fair,
Heartbeats echo, love is everywhere.

Stars peek through the ethereal veil,
Guiding spirits where the nightingale sail.
Elevating dreams on soft feathered wings,
In this realm, the soul truly sings.

Petals glisten with a dewdrop's kiss,
Serenity wrapped in a gentle bliss.
Waves of tranquility swirl around,
In Elysium, where pure hope is found.

Colors blend in a tapestry bright,
Where every shadow reveals the light.
Harmony flows like rivers so wide,
In Elysian realms, we choose to abide.

Thus, we wander through this endless dream,
Bathed in radiance, hearts agleam.
Forever embraced by the light's warm grace,
In Elysian realms, our sacred space.

Dreams Adrift on Cosmic Seas

On waves of stardust, we gently glide,
Through the vastness where the dreams reside.
Planets twirl in a cosmic ballet,
In the silence, our wishes play.

Galaxies shimmer in the velvet night,
Illuminating hopes with their radiant light.
Nebulae bloom in vibrant hues,
As we sail on, embracing the muse.

Our thoughts unspool like comet trails,
Charting courses in timeless tales.
In this expanse, we drift and soar,
Exploring wonders forevermore.

With every heartbeat, the universe sings,
Cosmic whispers weave through our wings.
Touched by the magic of astral seas,
We find our peace in celestial breeze.

Though anchored in this life below,
Our souls entwined with the astral flow.
Dreams adrift, a transcendent dance,
In cosmic seas, we take our chance.

Celestial Sighs

In twilight's glow, the stars align,
Whispers of the cosmos, soft and divine.
A lullaby from the heavens above,
Filling our hearts with celestial love.

Floating on currents of shimmering light,
We are cradled in the arms of the night.
Each twinkling beacon, a heartfelt sigh,
Telling tales that will never die.

With every breath, the universe flows,
In fragments of time, the wisdom grows.
Celestial echoes in our hearts reside,
Guiding our journey as we glide.

The moon whispers secrets, ancient and wise,
Wrapped in the glow of her tender guise.
We dance beneath her watchful gaze,
In the realm where time gently sways.

For in these moments, we transcend,
Boundless and free, with dreams to send.
Celestial sighs, a symphony sweet,
In the expanse where our spirits meet.

Comet's Veil

Through the night, a comet streaks bright,
Draped in a veil of shimmering light.
It carries our hopes on its fiery tail,
A fleeting journey, a timeless trail.

Across the canvas of the darkest sky,
Wishes take flight, unbound, they fly.
In its wake, dreams start to unfurl,
Stories of magic from a distant world.

As it dances on air, a shimmering spark,
Illuminating secrets hidden in the dark.
Guiding us onward with a radiant flare,
Comet's veil whispers of wonders rare.

In the shadow of night, it leaves its mark,
Casting enchantment where dreams embark.
From the mundane to realms of delight,
In the comet's embrace, we take flight.

With each passing moment, our spirits rise,
Chasing the echoes of the comet's cries.
Boundless and bright, we learn to unveil,
The magic of life in the comet's veil.

The Lonesome Traveler's Celestial Compass

Through valleys deep, the traveler roams,
Seeking stars like distant homes.
Each twinkling guide, a whisper, a call,
In the vast unknown, he hopes to find all.

Time is a river, flowing away,
With each night's fall, he begins to sway.
A compass of dreams, in the dark he'll trust,
For the heart knows the path, it must.

The mountains loom, shadows stretched wide,
Yet on he walks, with the moon as his guide.
Rivers sing tales of journeys begun,
Under the gaze of the watchful sun.

A lonesome figure beneath the vast sky,
Hoping for angels to hear his sigh.
In the silence, he crafts a prayer,
To the constellations, a love laid bare.

Embers of hope, like fireflies dance,
In the dreaming night, he finds romance.
With each gentle breeze, his spirit is free,
The compass spins true, just wait and see.

Celestial Symphonies of the Heart's Search

In the stillness of night, melodies weave,
Celestial notes in hearts that believe.
Each star a chord in the symphony bright,
Guiding lost souls toward the light.

With every heartbeat, the cosmos sings,
A rhythm of hope that eternity brings.
Where dreams intertwine with the pulse of the sea,
In the dance of the stars, we are truly free.

The moon whispers secrets in silvered tones,
Telling of journeys endured alone.
Yet in the vastness, connections emerge,
A harmony of souls where passions surge.

Light twirls around in a beautiful grace,
Touching the heart in an infinite space.
As the universe swells with each silent prayer,
Weaving together lives laid bare.

Through the cosmos, our spirits take flight,
Finding solace in the weave of the night.
In celestial symphonies, we come to trust,
The heart's endless search for the pure and just.

Chasing Stardust Through Infinite Skies

In the twilight's embrace, dreams take their flight,
Chasing the stardust, elusive and bright.
A canvas of night, where wishes are spun,
With each gentle breath, a new journey begun.

Through infinite skies, on the wings of the dawn,
He runs towards the light, never to yawn.
Every glimmer of hope is a beacon so dear,
Drawing him closer, undaunted by fear.

The universe hums with a mystical tune,
While hearts beat wildly beneath the pale moon.
Each star like a lighthouse, shimmering bold,
Guiding the seekers through stories untold.

In the dance of the orbs, he finds his way clear,
With every embrace, he sheds all his fear.
The vault of the heavens, a treasure to find,
In chasing the stardust, he leaves doubt behind.

As comets blaze trails, bursting with fire,
He knows in his heart, to dream is to aspire.
Through infinite skies, his spirit will soar,
For chasing the stardust is what he's made for.

The Light that Beckons Across Time

In the echoes of ages, a beacon does shine,
A light that reaches across the divine.
Through shadows of history, it calls out his name,
Awakening spirit, igniting the flame.

Each flicker a promise, a tale to unfold,
Of journeys of courage, of hearts growing bold.
Across endless moments, it weaves through the years,
In the fabric of time, it whispers our fears.

With footsteps of ancients, he walks in their wake,
Bound to the light, no path he will forsake.
In silence he listens, as wisdom unspools,
The past and the future, grand teachers, our schools.

The cosmos alight with intentions anew,
As stardust and dreams in the twilight accrue.
Each heartbeat a rhythm, a song deeply sung,
In the light that beckons, where all has begun.

Through valleys of time, he knows where to tread,
Guided by brilliance, no longer misled.
For the light that beckons will always remain,
A compass of hope on this journey through pain.

Ethereal Echoes of Wanderlust

In whispers soft, the winds do call,
A fleeting dream, we rise and fall.
With every step, the path unwinds,
The secrets that the heart still finds.

Through shadowed woods and starlit skies,
The distant tales of love arise.
Each echo speaks of what we seek,
In every moment, hope's unique.

The mountains high, the valleys low,
In wanderlust, our spirits grow.
With open hearts, we chase the dawn,
In every breath, a spark reborn.

As rivers flow and seasons turn,
The fires of passion brightly burn.
In every glance, a world unstayed,
In every journey, dreams are laid.

So let us roam the boundless air,
With open minds, beyond compare.
In ethereal whispers, we shall trust,
To find our way through wanderlust.

Horizon's Edge and the Glimpse of Gold

At horizon's edge, the sun dips low,
A canvas bright, where shadows glow.
With every hue, the day departs,
As twilight whispers to our hearts.

In gentle waves, the sea retreats,
With secrets held in rhythmic beats.
The glimmer soft on distant shores,
A promise wrapped in ocean roars.

As night unveils the stars so bold,
We glance at dreams that still unfold.
With every twinkle, hope ignites,
In moments shared beneath the lights.

The paths we walked, in sun and rain,
Each memory etched through joy and pain.
Beyond the clouds, our spirits soar,
In glimpses found, we crave for more.

So let us chase that golden gleam,
In every heart, a vibrant dream.
At horizon's edge, we'll find the light,
In every journey, day and night.

Journeying Toward the Eternal Flame

A flicker bright, the flame so true,
In every heart, a spark anew.
We journey forth, through trials vast,
In search of light that holds us fast.

With every step, the shadows creep,
Yet in our souls, a promise deep.
Through storms that roar, and nights so long,
We find the strength to carry on.

The flame ignites our hidden dreams,
In whispered words, the future gleams.
As we stride forth, hand in hand,
Together, bold, united we stand.

The paths may twist, the road may bend,
Yet in our hearts, we'll find the end.
As time unfolds, the flame will rise,
In each moment, our spirits fly.

So journey on, through light and dark,
With every step, we leave a mark.
Toward the flame that never wanes,
In love, we trust, through joys and pains.

Starbound Reflections from Within

In stillness deep, the night unfolds,
The cosmos vast, with dreams retold.
Each star a spark, a wish we share,
A mirror bright, in endless air.

From shadows cast, to light so pure,
Our souls reflect, forever sure.
In every twinkle, tales emerge,
Of journeys taken, hearts that surge.

As galaxies twirl in silent grace,
We find our home in time and space.
With every breath, the universe sighs,
In cosmic dance, our spirits rise.

In moments lost, we look within,
To seek the light where dreams begin.
As stardust whispers through the night,
Our inner world ignites with light.

So gaze upon the sky so wide,
With wonder deep, let hope abide.
For in the stars, our truths reside,
In starbound reflections, we confide.

Journeys Beyond the Milky Way

Beyond the stars, where dreams reside,
We sail on ships that never hide.
Whispers of dusk, the cosmos sings,
As vast as hope, as light takes wings.

Galaxies spin in a cosmic waltz,
Beckoning souls, it never halts.
In stardust trails, we find our way,
Through galaxies bright, we choose to stay.

Nebulae glow in colors bright,
Each one a tale of ancient night.
Through cosmic seas we wander far,
Guided only by a distant star.

With every pulse of the silent space,
We challenge time, we echo grace.
Adventures grand in twilight's hue,
Our journey starts with dreams anew.

So let us leap into the night,
For in this dark, we find the light.
Together woven in love, we play,
In journeys bold, beyond the Milky Way.

The Allure of the Infinite Sky

A canvas wide, of endless blue,
Where scattered dreams are born anew.
Beneath the deep, where wonders lie,
We gaze in awe at the infinite sky.

Twinkling lights, like whispered prayers,
Each one a wish that softly stares.
Embracing galaxies, bold and bright,
We wander through the wondrous night.

Constellations tell of ancient lore,
Drawing our hearts to seek for more.
In that expanse, our spirits fly,
Chasing the glow of the endless sky.

Shooting stars leave traces behind,
In fleeting glances, beauty aligned.
We chase our dreams with hearts so spry,
Entranced forever by the infinite sky.

Here in the depths of night, we're free,
In this grand dance of eternity.
With every breath, we learn to sigh,
For love is born beneath the infinite sky.

A Dance Among the Stars

In the stillness of the night, we sway,
A dance of shadows where dreams play.
Among the stars, we leap and glide,
With every heartbeat, our souls collide.

The rhythm echoes through the galaxies far,
Each twirl and twist, a guiding star.
We spin through orbits and cosmic beams,
Lost in the beauty of endless dreams.

Nebulas shimmer, they start to glow,
As we embrace the starlit flow.
With every step, the cosmos sings,
In harmony, our spirits take wings.

A melody bright, in the celestial night,
Through silken shadows, we find our light.
Together in space, we laugh and dance,
In the galaxy's embrace, we take our chance.

No limits, no bounds—just joy, just stars,
In this vast expanse, we forget our scars.
Within the universe, we forge our fate,
In the dance of the stars, we celebrate.

Twilight's Fading Glow

As twilight falls with a gentle sigh,
The sun dips low, painting the sky.
Colors blend in a soft embrace,
A fading glow, a tranquil space.

The whispering winds carry secrets old,
In dusky hues, their stories told.
Stars awaken, one by one,
In the quiet night, the day is done.

Moonlight drips like liquid silver,
Casting dreams that make us shiver.
In shadows deep, we find our peace,
With each heartbeat, our worries cease.

Crickets sing in a soft refrain,
Reminding us of love's sweet gain.
In twilight's arms, we find our flow,
Lost in the beauty of fading glow.

As night unfolds with a velvet grace,
We cherish moments we can't replace.
In every dusk, a promise shows,
A tomorrow bright, though twilight glows.

Navigating by Night

Under the stars that gleam,
We sail through dreams unseen.
Shadows whisper tales of old,
Guiding hearts that brave and bold.

The moon casts silver on the sea,
A beacon for the lost to be.
With each wave, a secret shared,
In the night, we're unprepared.

Yet courage rises with the tide,
The compass within, a loyal guide.
Through the darkness, we will steer,
To shores where hope draws near.

Each sigh of wind, a silent prayer,
In the depths, we cast our care.
Navigating by the light,
We journey on, into the night.

With every star's embrace, we find,
A path that lingers in the mind.
In silent waters, dreams ignite,
As we keep sailing, by night.

Beyond the Veil of Darkness

In the quiet, shadows creep,
Where secrets lie and whispers weep.
Beyond the veil, the truth awaits,
In hidden realms, we open gates.

A fragile light begins to shine,
Illuminating paths divine.
As we venture through the night,
The heart will guide, the soul takes flight.

In depths where fears are chained,
Strength emerges, hope unrestrained.
With every step, we dare to trust,
Beyond the darkness, rise we must.

Through trials faced and lessons learned,
Wisdom in every corner turned.
The night conceals but also shows,
A brighter dawn that subtly grows.

So let us tread with cautious grace,
In shadows find our rightful place.
For beyond the veil of dark despair,
Awaits the light we long to share.

Echoes of a Shining Path

Whispers dance upon the breeze,
Tales of courage carried far, with ease.
The trail we walk, a glowing thread,
Echoes of the dreams we've shed.

In the distance, colors blend,
A canvas bright that never ends.
Footsteps echo, soft and clear,
A journey led by love and fear.

Through valleys deep and mountains tall,
We rise, we stumble, yet we call.
For every challenge faced with might,
Becomes a star that fills the night.

In the echoes, stories weave,
Of all the moments we believe.
With every turn, new paths arise,
Illuminating all our skies.

So let us walk this shining path,
In unity, we'll find the math.
Together, weaving dreams we craft,
In echoes sweet, our souls are daft.

Lustrous Whispers Above

In twilight's glow, the stars appear,
Lustrous whispers, soft and clear.
Each flicker tells a tale of old,
In their embrace, the night unfolds.

As shadows stretch into the night,
Hearts awaken, seeking light.
The heavens pulse with secret grace,
Guiding lost souls to their place.

With every twinkle, a wish takes flight,
Spirits rushing through the night.
In the vastness, hope ignites,
Painting dreams with cosmic lights.

Together, beneath this sky,
We find the courage to fly high.
In whispers, love is softly spoken,
Binding souls, unbroken, unbroken.

So let us gaze and feel this warmth,
In lustrous night, our hearts transform.
With every star, a promise reigns,
In whispers above, forever gains.

Seeking Light's Embrace

In quiet shadows, I roam free,
Hoping to find what's meant for me.
A flicker here, a shimmer there,
The warmth of hope fills the air.

Through tangled woods, beneath the stars,
I search for love that heals the scars.
With every step, light draws me near,
A beacon bright, devoid of fear.

Each whispered breeze calls out my name,
In dreams, I chase an endless flame.
The heart ignites, the spirit sings,
As joy unfolds on tender wings.

Rays of dawn come breaking through,
Painting the sky in vibrant hue.
I hold my breath, embrace the light,
And let my soul take joyful flight.

Together we'll dance, you and I,
In the embrace of the open sky.
In seeking light, I've found my way,
A heart reborn, ready to stay.

Whispering Galaxies

In the silent night, stars align,
Whispers of galaxies intertwine.
A cosmic dance, a gentle sway,
Lost in wonder, I drift away.

The moonlight glows, soft and serene,
Painting the world in silver sheen.
With every twinkle, tales unfold,
Ancient stories in stardust told.

Nebulas swirl in colors bright,
Echoes of dreams in the velvet night.
I reach for the heavens, hand above,
Craving the light, the pulse of love.

Time stands still as I gaze above,
In the embrace of the universe's love.
Galaxies whisper their sacred song,
In their vastness, I know I belong.

Through endless nights, I seek the spark,
Navigating tides, igniting the dark.
In the depths of space, I find my voice,
In whispering galaxies, I rejoice.

Dance of Celestial Bodies

Planets twirl in a cosmic ballet,
Choreographed in a grand display.
Stars spin gently in the sky's embrace,
In the vast expanse, they find their place.

The sun ignites the dawn with fire,
A dance of light, taking us higher.
With every rotation, a promise made,
In the rhythm of time, dreams never fade.

Comets streak across the night's canvas,
Painting the silence with their fervor.
In wondrous arcs, they chase the moon,
In the dance of life, we find our tune.

The universe whispers, secrets unfurl,
In this grand show, we all have a role.
Gravitation pulls at my heart,
In the dance of bodies, I become a part.

Embracing the space where shadows play,
I lose myself in the vast array.
Celestial bodies, forever they spin,
In the dance of the cosmos, we begin.

The Yearn for Illumination

In a world wrapped in twilight's cloak,
A whisper of light is what I invoke.
The heart seeks truth, a guiding flame,
In shadows deep, it calls my name.

A flicker glows in the depths of night,
Illuminating paths hidden from sight.
Every step forward, with courage I take,
Embracing the dawn, for hope's own sake.

In moments of silence, wisdom flows,
In the quest for light, my spirit grows.
Each ray that breaks the darkened gloom,
Turns barren spaces to vibrant bloom.

With every sunrise, the day begins,
A tapestry woven with love and sins.
I yearn for clarity, a softer touch,
In the arms of light, it means so much.

Through valleys low and peaks so high,
I chase the brightness across the sky.
In the yearn for illumination, I find
The beauty of life, and peace of mind.

www.ingramcontent.com/pod-product-compliance
Ingram Content Group UK Ltd.
Pitfield, Milton Keynes, MK11 3LW, UK
UKHW022039040225
4445UKWH00034B/410